A LITTLE IRISH

Book of Days

Appletree Press

In January if the sun appear
March and April pay full dear.

JANUARY

1

2

JANUARY

3

4

5

6

7

Mayo Moon

In County Mayo, the first new moon of the New Year was used in a marriage divination ceremony. The man who wished to dream of his future partner knelt down, picked up a handful of clay and said:

New moon, true moon, new moon trick,
Bring to me my true love quick,
The colour of her hair, the clothes she'll wear;
And may appear to me this night in my dream,
And the day she'll be, married to me.

JANUARY

8

9

10

11

12

May there be a fox on your fishing-hook
And a hare on your bait
And may you kill no fish until St Brigid's Day.

JANUARY

13

14

JANUARY

15

16

17

18

19

Dublin Coddle

A very popular dish, especially in Dublin. It is nourishing, tasty, economical and warming.

8 oz/250 g streaky bacon	6 medium potatoes
1/2 pt/300 ml/1 cup stock or water	2 medium onions
1 lb /500 g best sausages	salt and pepper

Cut the bacon into 1 in/3 cm squares. Bring the stock to the boil in a medium saucepan which has a well-fitting lid, add the sausages and the bacon and simmer for about 5 minutes. Remove the sausages and bacon and save liquid. Cut each sausage into four or five pieces. Peel the potatoes and cut into thick slices. Skin the onions and slice them. Assemble a layer of potatoes in the saucepan, followed by a layer of onions and then half the sausages and bacon. Repeat the process once more and then finish off with a layer of potatoes. Pour the reserved stock over and season lightly to taste. Cover and simmer gently for about an hour.

JANUARY

20

21

22

23

24

A misty winter brings a pleasant spring,
A pleasant winter a misty spring.

JANUARY

25

26

JANUARY

27

28

29

30

31

St Brigid's Day

The feast of St Brigid (Feb. 1) appears to be a christianisation of one the focal points of the Irish agricultural year: the first day of spring and the beginning of the farming cycle, when many farmers went out into the fields and symbolically began the year's work by turning a sod or two. There are many customs attached to St Brigid's Day. Legend has it that one day Brigid was at the deathbed of an old pagan chieftain to whom she tried in vain to explain the gospels. As she sat on the rush-covered floor she picked up a bunch of rushes and began to weave a cross. She showed it to the chieftain and was able to convert him to the Christian faith just before he died. Since then, on the eve of her feast, people make these crosses to hang in their houses and on byres as a protection against evil.

FEBRUARY

1

2

3

4

5

February fill the dyke
Be it black or be it white.

FEBRUARY

FEBRUARY

8

9

10

11

12

Hot Whiskey

A favourite winter drink in Irish pubs, hot whiskey is also known as 'hot Irish' or just 'punch'.

---

boiling water
1-2 tsp sugar
1 large measure Irish whiskey
slice of lemon
2 or 3 whole cloves

Warm a stemmed whiskey glass with very hot water. Pour in fresh boiling water to more than half full, and sugar to taste. Stir to dissolve the sugar, add a good measure of whiskey, a slice of lemon and the cloves. Serve at once.

FEBRUARY

13

14

15

16

17

May you have warm words on a cold evening,
A full moon on a dark night;
And the road downhill all the way to your door.

FEBRUARY

18

19

FEBRUARY

20

21

22

23

24

Shrove Tuesday

Shrovetide is the traditional time for marriages in rural Ireland, a custom which seems to have evolved from the prohibition of the sacrament of matrimony during the Lenten season. Conversely, it was taken for granted that those who did not marry at this time did not intend to do so that year, this being generally regarded as a neglect of social duty. In Munster and parts of Leinster, the Sunday following Shrove Tuesday was known as 'Chalk Sunday', when those who remained unmarried at Shrove often had their clothes decorated with chalk marks by young boys and girls, a cause of particular irritation to hardened old bachelors.

FEBRUARY

25

26

27

28

29

March – in like a lion
and out like a lamb.

MARCH

1

2

MARCH

3

4

5

6

7

Brotchán Foltchep

Leeks have been mentioned in literature since early times, usually in connection with Lent. This is a traditional Irish leek and oatmeal soup.

---

2 pt milk
2 oz oatmeal
knob of butter
2 lb leeks
salt and pepper
parsley

Boil the milk with the oatmeal until cooked. Add the butter and mix in the chopped leeks, cool gently for one hour. Season to taste and garnish with chopped parsley.

MARCH

8

9

10

11

12

St Patrick was a gentleman
Who through strategy and stealth
Drove all the snakes from Ireland,
Here's a toasting to his health!

MARCH

15

16

17

18

19

Spring Sowing

In March farmers turned their attention to spring sowing. One custom associated with it involved the horses in the ploughing team being 'turned with the sun' at the end of the furrow; the sower then blessed the work in the name of the Trinity, and tossed a handful of soil over each horse's rump. St Patrick's Day was thought propitious for sowing the first potatoes, and even better results might be obtained if this coincided with the period of a waxing moon. In the north of Ireland it was the custom to sow seed with the left hand from a bedsheet clasped over the right shoulder. No piece of ground was missed, for if this happened a death would take place on the farm within a year.

MARCH

20

21

22

23

24

Sow early and mow early.

MARCH

25

26

MARCH

27

28

29

30

31

April Fool

The custom of making a fool of somebody on the first day of April can be traced back to at least the early eighteenth century. In Ireland a favourite prank was that of 'sending the fool farther'. One way to do this was to send a child to a neighbour's house to borrow a glass hammer. The child was told that it had been given to some other neighbour and that he should call at his house. The prank continued as long as the naive child allowed it, or until some neighbour took pity on him and sent him home.

APRIL

1

2

3

4

5

April showers
Bring forth May flowers.

APRIL

|6|

|7|

APRIL

8

9

10

11

12

Bookie's Sandwich

This sandwich is often taken to race meetings, or on shoots.

---

bread
butter
$^1/_2$ lb/250 g steak
mustard

Butter two thick slices of bread. Fry the steak and place it on one of the slices. Spread with mustard and season to taste. Place the other slice on top and allow to cool under a light weight. Keep wrapped until ready to eat.

APRIL

13

14

15

16

17

May the grass grow long
On the road to hell
For want of use.
APRIL

18

19

APRIL

20

21

22

23

24

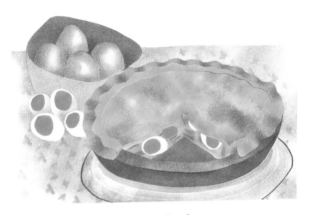

Donegal Pie

This is a very filling pie for hard-working people. The recipe comes from the north-west corner of Ireland.

> 2 lb/1 kg mashed potatoes
> 2 hard-boiled eggs
> $^1/_2$ lb/250 g bacon
> $^1/_2$ lb/250 g pastry

Grease the pie dish and half fill it with potatoes. Slice the eggs and place on top. Fry the bacon until crisp, then place on top of the eggs and pour over the bacon fat. Cover with the rest of the potatoes. Make a pastry lid and bake in a hot oven for about $1^1/_2$ hours.

APRIL

25

26

27

28

29

A wet and windy May
Fills the barns with oats and hay.

APRIL–MAY

30

1

MAY

2

3

4

5

6

Hiring Fairs

Hiring fairs were often held in conjunction with cattle fairs in May. Farmers who could not afford paid labour all year round hired workers for the busy summer months. In West Cork, Kerry, and parts of Connacht, many young men left home in early spring to walk to the fairs in the Midlands, and some travelled further afield to England and Scotland. These were the 'spalpíni' (spalpeens) who often did not return home until after the October potato harvest. Those seeking work sometimes wore a token of their particular skill: the shepherd carried his crook or wore a twist of sheep-wool on his cap; the carter decorated his hat with a piece of whipcord; and the dairy maid carried her milking stool. An exchange also took place when the working contract had been agreed: the employer handed over 'earles' or earnest money to his newly-hired labour, while the hireling handed over his bundle of clothes as a token of good faith.

MAY

7

8

9

10

11

The health of the salmon to you,
A long life, a full heart
And a wet mouth.

MAY

MAY

14

15

16

17

18

Baked Salmon

There is no doubt that this is an expensive dish, but it will feed eight to ten people and makes a fine party piece.

1 whole fresh salmon (about 5 lb/2 kg)	4 oz/125 g/^{1}/$_2$ cup butter
parsley	^{1}/$_4$ pt/125 ml/^{1}/$_2$ cup dry cider
salt and pepper	^{1}/$_2$ pt/250 ml/1 cup double cream

Clean and descale the salmon, cut off the head and tail and trim the fins. Stuff the parsley into the gullet. Butter some aluminium foil and form a loose envelope round the fish, sealing both ends but leaving the top open for the moment. Dot the rest of the butter over the salmon, season and pour over the cider and the cream. Now seal the foil along the top, leaving only a small vent. Bake in the oven for 1^1/$_4$ hours at gas mark 4, 350°F, 180°C. When ready, take from the oven, remove the skin and reduce the sauce by boiling, stirring all the time. Serve with boiled new potatoes and fresh garden peas.

MAY

19

20

21

22

23

May the Lord keep you in His hand
And never close His fist too tight on you.

MAY

24

25

MAY

26

27

28

29

30

Irish Coffee

This heady mixture of cream, coffee and Irish whiskey was invented by a chef at Shannon Airport who felt that arriving travellers could do with a warm, comforting drink.

---

³/4 cup hot, strong, black coffee
1-2 tsp sugar
1 large measure Irish whiskey
1-2 tbsp double cream

Fill a stemmed whiskey glass with hot water then throw out, refilling it with boiling water. Throw this out, fill the glass somewhat more than half full with coffee and add sugar to taste. Stir to dissolve, then add the whiskey. Pour the cream over the back of a spoon to float on top. Drink the hot liquid through the cool cream. If double cream is not available use lightly-whipped single (whipping) cream.

MAY–JUNE

31

1

2

3

4

A drop of rain in June
Makes the farmer whistle a merry tune.

JUNE

5

6

JUNE

7

8

9

10

11

Boxty in the Pan

Boxty is a traditional potato dish, celebrated in the rhyme: 'Boxty on the griddle, Boxty in the pan, If you can't make boxty, You'll never get your man.'

---

8 oz/250 g/2 cups raw potato	1 tsp baking powder
8 oz/250 g/2 cups mashed potato	1 tsp salt
8 oz/250 g/2 cups plain flour	large knob of butter, melted
about $^1/_4$ pt/125 ml/$^1/_2$ cup milk or buttermilk	

Peel the raw potatoes and grate them onto a linen teatowel. Squeeze and collect the liquid in a basin, and leave to stand. Mix the grated potatoes and the mashed potatoes. When the starch has separated from the liquid, pour off the water and add the starch to the potatoes. Add the dry ingredients and mix well, then add enough buttermilk to form a dropping consistency. Beat well and leave to stand a little before frying in spoonfuls in a greased pan. Fry on both sides and serve with butter and sugar.

JUNE

12

13

14

15

16

May the strength of three
Be in your journey.

JUNE

JUNE

19

20

21

22

23

Midsummer Day

Midsummer Day was the occasion for festival and sacrifice in pre-Christian times, and its eve a night for bonfires, which were thought to keep at bay malevolent forces particularly potent at this period. The popular custom of 'leaping over the bonfire', possibly the relic of an earlier purification rite, in which a path was made through the centre of the fire by moving the embers to either side, took place on Midsummer Eve. Young men and women competed with each other to see who could leap the highest over the flames, and whoever jumped the highest would be the first to marry. Another custom involved taking a glowing ember from the fire and carrying it three times around the house: this ensured a household free from illness for the following year. In fact, bonfires were so popular on Midsummer Eve that if you stood on a hilltop a hundred years ago and looked in any direction, you could have seen fires burning on almost every hill.

JUNE

24

25

26

27

28

A swarm of bees in July
Isn't worth a butterfly.

JUNE

29

30

JULY

1

2

3

4

5

The Hungry Month

The period preceding the harvest was one of anxiety for farmers and sometimes of tragedy for poor people with no land or cattle. The six weeks between Midsummer and the end of July were known as 'the bitter six weeks', and July itself as 'the hungry month' or 'the month of shaking out of bags'. At this time, the bags containing the last remnants of flour and meal from the previous year's harvest were shaken out, the last scraps used, and the bags laid ready for the new season. Potatoes were, of course, the foremost crop, and by July, the previous year's supply was almost exhausted, while the new crop would not ripen until the end of the month. Hence the saying in Co. Waterford:

> July of the cabbage,
> July of the onion dip,
> August of the new potatoes.

JULY

6

7

8

9

10

Here's that we may always have
A clean shirt, a clean conscience
And a guinea in our pocket.

JULY

11

12

JULY

13

14

15

16

17

Boiled Bacon and Cabbage

Cabbage is a favourite vegetable in Ireland and probably the most widely used. 'White' cabbage is pale in colour and tightly leaved: this variety will stand the long cooking of boiled meat dishes.

---

2 lb/1 kg piece of boiling bacon
water
1 large cabbage

Place the bacon in a saucepan. Cover with water and bring to the boil. Simmer for about two hours, or until tender. Remove the bacon, slice the cabbage and add to the water. Boil for about ten minutes, keeping the bacon warm. Slice the bacon, drain the cabbage and serve.

JULY

18

19

20

21

22

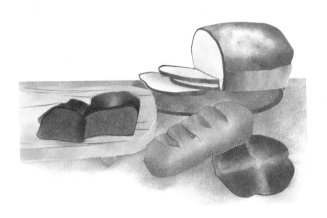

Rye bread will do you good
Barley bread will do you no harm,
Wheaten bread will sweeten your blood,
Oaten bread will strengthen your arm.

JULY

25

26

27

28

29

Lammas Fairs

The first day of August is known as Lammas Day, a derivation from the Anglo-Saxon 'halfmaesse' or 'loaf mass', the feast day on which bread for the Sacrament was made from newly-ripened corn. In early Celtic communities the festival of Lughnasa, held at the same time of the year in honour of the god Lugh, coincided with the harvest. Over time, with the christianization of Ireland, these celebrations became merged with the Lammas fairs which were held in towns all over the country. The most famous two still held are the Puck Fair in Co. Kerry and the Lammas Fair in Ballycastle, Co. Antrim, the latter being well-known not only for pony and cattle sales, but also for its market stalls selling a wide range of goods, notably dulse, the seaweed delicacy, and the sticky sweet, 'yellow man'.

30

31

1

2

3

Dry August and warm
Does harvest no harm.

AUGUST

5

AUGUST

6

7

8

9

10

The Puck Fair

The Puck Fair at Killorglin in Co. Kerry takes place over three days. The first is known as the 'gathering day', the second as 'fair day', and the last 'scattering day'. Primarily a livestock fair, it is also a meeting place for the travelling people of Ireland, and has recently been swollen out of all proportion by tourists. On the evening of 'gathering day' the 'poc' or he-goat is dressed with ribbons and hoisted into his cage high above the crowd. Here 'King Puck' presides over the three days of the celebrations, a custom said to commemorate a warning, given by goats, of the advance of a hostile army on Killorglin. It is likely that the Puck is a symbol of the fair, in much the same way that, at others, a white horse or a pair of gloves on a pole signified that those who wished to trade might do so.

AUGUST

11

12

13

14

15

May the roof above us never fall in,
And may we friends gathered below
Never fall out.

AUGUST

AUGUST

18

19

20

21

22

Yellowman

This is a toothsome, honeycombed, sticky toffee traditionally sold at the Lammas Fair in Ballycastle, County Antrim at the end of August.

---

1 lb/¹/₂ kg/1¹/₂ cups golden or corn syrup
8 oz/250 g/1 cup brown sugar
1 tbsp butter (heaped)
2 tbsp vinegar
1 tsp baking soda

In a large saucepan slowly melt together all the ingredients except the baking soda. Do not stir. Boil until a drop hardens in cold water (240°F, 190°C on a sugar thermometer). Stir in the baking soda. The toffee will immediately foam up as the vinegar releases the gas from the baking soda. Pour out onto a greased slab and, when just cool enough to handle, fold the edges towards the centre and pull repeatedly until the whole is a pale yellow colour. Allow to cool and harden in a greased tin and break into chunks with a toffee hammer – or anything else that comes to hand.

AUGUST

23

24

25

26

27

September blow soft
Till fruit be in the loft.

AUGUST

28

29

AUGUST-SEPTEMBER

30

31

1

2

3

The Harvest Home

September usually saw the end of the harvest period. Since corn used to be the most important crop, the last sheaf of corn to be cut was the symbol of the end of the harvest. In Ulster, the workers threw their reaping hooks at it. In other parts of Ireland the owner of the field was blindfolded and had to crawl on his hands and knees, find the sheaf and cut it. The successful gathering of the harvest was followed by a 'harvest home', a feast given by the farmer for his workers. The smaller farms in the north and west usually held it in the kitchen while the larger farms of the south and east held it in the great corn barn, which would have been cleared and filled with rows of tables on the previous day. The meal usually consisted of sides of bacon and rounds and ribs of beef, accompanied by cabbage, potatoes and jugs of home-brewed beer. This was followed by a dance at which the girl who had tied the last sheaf was led out first by the farmer or his eldest son.

SEPTEMBER

4

5

6

7

8

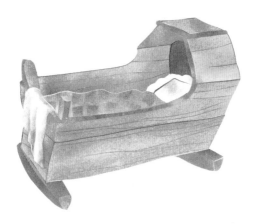

May there be a generation of children
On the children of your children.

SEPTEMBER

9

10

SEPTEMBER

11

12

13

14

15

Black Caps

Apples grow well in Ireland and the first windfalls of the autumn make a delicious dessert.

---

18 pippins
juice and rind of a lemon
2 tbsp orange flower water
$^1/_2$ lb sugar

Halve the apples. Set them together, cut side down, in a dish. Pour the lemon juice, rind and orange flower water over them. Sprinkle with sugar, and bake in a moderate oven for half an hour.

SEPTEMBER

16

17

18

19

20

Praise the ripe field, not the green corn.

SEPTEMBER

21

22

SEPTEMBER

23

24

25

26

27

Michaelmas

The feast of St Michael the Archangel on September 29 was traditionally one of the most important days of the year. It was generally considered that the summer season ended at Michaelmas, hence the saying, 'Summer is summer till Michaelmas Day'. A fine spell of weather at the end of September was called a Michaelmas Summer.

The best remembered custom connected with Michaelmas was the eating of the Michaelmas Goose. A goose was usually chosen well before the feast, and specially fed to fatten it. It was killed on Michaelmas Eve, and some of its blood was sprinkled on the threshold and at the four corners of the house. This was usually done by the woman of the house, and was thought to keep sickness and accidents away during the following year. The rest of the blood was mixed with chopped onion, breadcrumbs, herbs and spices, and boiled in a muslin bag, and the resulting pudding eaten with the roast goose.

28

29

30

1

2

There are always twenty-one
fine days in October.

OCTOBER

3

4

OCTOBER

5

6

7

8

9

Guinness Cake

This cake is quickly and easily made and, though it tastes good fresh from the oven, is best kept for about a week in an airtight tin.

1/4 lb/125 g/1/2 cup mixed peel	1/2 lb/250 g/1 cup butter
1/4 lb/125 g/1/2 cup almonds	1 lb/1/2 kg/4 cups flour
pinch nutmeg	1 lb/1/2 kg/2 cups sugar
1 bottle Guinness	11/2 lb/1 kg/5 cups dried fruit
1 lemon	1 tsp baking soda
4 eggs	1/4 lb/125 g/1/2 cup cherries

Rub the butter into the flour. Mix well with the dry ingredients. Add the Guinness, lemon juice and beaten eggs. Bake in an 8-inch tin in a slow oven for about three hours.

OCTOBER

10

11

12

13

14

May I see you grey
And combing your children's hair.

OCTOBER

16

OCTOBER

17

18

19

20

21

Hallowe'en

Hallowe'en, one of the most important and best kept of all the fire feasts, is celebrated at what was once the beginning of the Celtic year. Kindling bonfires is still popular at Hallowe'en, although few people today associate them with their original purpose which, as with many other Hallowe'en customs, was aimed at protecting people from the evil forces particularly potent at this time of the year. Those assembled around the fires would throw the lighted embers about in all directions in an attempt to purify themselves and ward off evil spirits. Similarly, the masks worn at today's bonfire parties are a relic of those days when grotesque disguises hid the true identities of people from any witch or warlock that might wish them harm.

OCTOBER

22

23

24

25

26

If there is ice in November
That will bear a duck,
There'll be nothing left but sludge and muck.

OCTOBER

27

28

29

30

31

1

2

All Souls' Day

Between Hallowe'en and All Souls' Day (2 November) customs centred on death, and on the festival of All Souls itself prayers were recited for the repose of the souls of the dead. Dead members of the family were thought to return to visit their old home on this night, and care was taken to show that they were welcome. The family retired to bed early, leaving the door unlatched, a good fire burning in the hearth, and the table laid with a place for each of its dead members.

NOVEMBER

3

4

5

6

7

May you live to be a hundred years,
With one extra year to repent.

NOVEMBER

 8

9

NOVEMBER

10

11

12

13

14

Irish Stew

If made with mutton and cooked slowly, this hearty, nourishing and traditional dish will be both flavoursome and tender.

2 lb/1 kg boned mutton	sprig of parsley
4 large potatoes	1 pt/500 ml/2 cups water
2 large onions	salt and pepper
3 or 4 medium carrots	

Cut the meat into good-sized chunks. Peel the vegetables and slice thickly. Chop the parsley. Choose a pot with a well-fitting lid and put in the ingredients in layers, starting and finishing with potatoes. Pour in the water and season to taste. Cover and put on a very low heat for about 2¹/₂ hours until the meat is tender and the potatoes have thickened the liquid. The dish may also be made with lamb, in which case it requires only 1¹/₂ hours cooking time.

NOVEMBER

15

16

17

18

19

A little fire that warms
Is better than a big fire that burns.

NOVEMBER

20

21

NOVEMBER

22

23

24

25

26

Christmas Preparations

People hoped for snow over this time, because of the proverb, 'A green Christmas makes a fat churchyard.' But the month of December was a cheery one which saw the start of preparations for Christmas. For most people, Christmas really began weeks in advance and trips to the local town were made to buy dried fruit, candles, drink, spices, tobacco and clothes. Country people bought butter, fowl, eggs and vegetables to town markets to sell and to do their own shopping with the proceeds. Christmas trees and Christmas cards, customs introduced in Victorian times, were bought and cribs, symbolising the birth of Jesus, made and lit by the Christmas candle.

NOVEMBER–DECEMBER

27

28

29

30

1

Marry when December's snow falls fast
Always joy and true love will last.

DECEMBER

2

3

DECEMBER

4

5

6

7

8

Spiced Beef

Spiced beef is traditionally eaten at Christmas time. It tends to be rather expensive to buy already made as it is quite labour intensive, though it uses a modestly-priced cut.

7 lb/3 kg even-sized piece
of topside or silverside
2 tsp each ground cloves,
milled black pepper,
allspice, cinnamon, mace
and saltpetre

2 tbsp black treacle
2 tbsp brown sugar
cold water to cover
bottle of Guinness
$^1/_2$ cup salt

Combine all the ingredients except the beef, water and Guinness. Place the beef in a bowl and cover with the mixture. Rub it in once or twice a day for a week. Tie up the meat into a good shape and place in a pan. Cover with cold water to which the bottle of Guinness has been added. Simmer gently for 5-6 hours. When cool, press lightly between two plates. The beef is usually served cold, thinly sliced.

DECEMBER

9

10

11

12

13

Wide is the door of the little cottage.

DECEMBER

14

15

DECEMBER

16

17

18

19

20

Christmas

In pre-Christian times, this was the ancient mid-winter solstice. During the Roman festival of Saturnalia, the temples were decorated with greenery and the traditional Irish practice of decorating the house with holly and ivy may stem from this. Mistletoe was also used as a decoration or 'kissing bough', especially in Counties Wicklow and Armagh. While Christmas Eve was a fast day with no meat, Christmas Day dinner was the most important meal of the year. Boiled or roast beef was the most popular Christmas fare, although in parts of Leinster and Munster goose was eaten. In the evening, the Christmas cake was cut and spicy mince pies eaten: if you could eat a mince pie for each of the twelve days of Christmas you might have a year free from illness!

DECEMBER

21

22

23

24

25

In the New Year, may your right hand always
Be stretched out in friendship and never in want.

DECEMBER

26

27

DECEMBER–JANUARY

28

29

30

31

1

Acknowledgements

Grateful acknowledgement is made to the Department of Irish Folklore, University College Dublin, for permission to reproduce proverbs, and to George McClafferty for permission to reproduce accounts of folk customs.

First published by The Appletree Press Ltd, 7 James Street South, Belfast, BT2 8DL. Copyright © The Appletree Press Ltd, 1991, 1992. All rights reserved. No part of this publication may be reproduced or transmitted in any form or by any means, electronic or mechanical, photocopying, recording or any information and retrieval system, without permission in writing from The Appletree Press Ltd.

Printed in the E.C.